POET TOWERS

HIDDEN TREASURES

EDITED BY WENDY LAWS

First published in Great Britain in 2023 by:

YoungWriters®
Est. 1991

Young Writers
Remus House
Coltsfoot Drive
Peterborough
PE2 9BF
Telephone: 01733 890066
Website: www.youngwriters.co.uk

All Rights Reserved
Book Design by Ashley Janson
© Copyright Contributors 2023
Softback ISBN 978-1-80459-751-4

Printed and bound in the UK by BookPrintingUK
Website: www.bookprintinguk.com
YB0556D

FOREWORD

For Young Writers' latest competition we invited primary school pupils to enroll at a new school, Poetry Towers, where they could let their imaginations roam free.

At Poetry Towers the timetable of subjects on offer is unlimited, so pupils could choose any topic that inspired them and write in any poetry style. We provided free resources including lesson plans, poetry guides and inspiration and examples to help pupils craft a piece of writing they can be proud of.

Here at Young Writers our aim is to encourage creativity in children and to inspire a love of the written word, so it's great to get such an amazing response, with some absolutely fantastic poems. It's important for children to express themselves and a great way to engage them is to allow them to write about what they care about. The result is a varied collection of poems with a range of styles and techniques that showcase their creativity and writing ability.

We'd like to congratulate all the young poets in this anthology, the latest alumni of the Young Writers' academy of poetry and rhyme. We hope this inspires them to continue with their creative writing.

CONTENTS

Clifton Hall School, Newbridge

Zara Finlay (8)	1
Thomas Adams (8)	2
Sophia Duffie (8)	3
Rose Bertile (9)	4
Rose Butlin (9)	5
Cara Woolley (8)	6
Emily McKay (8)	7
Farrah Youssef (8)	8
Austin Gunn (8)	9
Varshika Ganapathiran Sivakamini (8)	10
Cole Thomson (8)	11
Cameron McKeown (9)	12
Solomon Bisi-Olaitan (8)	13
Stephen Hodgson (8)	14
Jamie Kadzimu (8)	15
Noah Dryburgh-Cook (8)	16
Ryan Timmins (8)	17
Elspeth Stewart (8)	18

Downfield Primary School, Cheshunt

Emilija Stepanova (9)	19
Lauma Pilka (10)	20
Joseph Morrison (10)	21
Sophie Butcher (9)	22
Emily Lugg (10)	23
Talulah Sambrook (10)	24
Elif Demikiran (10)	25
Zoe Ma (9)	26
Maia Gustavsson (10)	27
Rogue Jacks (10)	28
Florence Smith (10)	29

Charlie Knipes (9)	30
Chloe Bennett (10)	31
Sienna Edwards (10)	32
Harry Bennett (10)	33
Lucy Roe (10)	34
Diego Sacko (10)	35
Eron Xhemshiti (10)	36
Yuina Honda (10)	37
Riley Phillips (10)	38

Etching Hill Primary School, Etching Hill

Aria Holland (10)	39
Amber Laud (10)	40
Virginia Maduakor (10)	42
Chloe Bateman (10)	44
Connor Stevenson (10)	46
Victoria Sopron (10)	48
Oscar Harwood (10)	50
Daniel Liddle (10)	52
Freya Vukmirovic (10)	54
Rosie Jackson (10)	56
Isobel S-B (10)	58
Georgia Bott (10)	60
Alexia Wharton (10)	62
Emilia Halberda (10)	63

Haughton St Giles CE Primary Academy, Haughton

Imogen Mills (10)	65
Esmee Whittingham (8)	66
Victoria Kolasa (9)	67
Marley Hague (9)	68
Phoebe Widger (10)	69

Boris Hubev (8)	70
Eva Lamont (8)	71
Davie Willmott (9)	72
Jayden Edwards (8)	73
Layla Brain (8)	74
Izabela Hubeva (10)	75
Seren Abell (8)	76
Grace Wardell (11)	77
George Gardiner (8)	78
Emelia Allen (11)	79

Inkberrow Primary School, Inkberrow

Lily Parnell (9)	80
Isla Taylor (9)	81
Florence White (9)	82
Olivia Seal (9)	83

Lancing Prep At Worthing, Worthing

Eileen Chapman (9)	84
Elliott Sandell (9)	86
Eithne Wallace Nannig (9)	87
Autumn Shore (8)	88
Amalie Subedar (9)	89
Elodie Gibbs (9)	90
Hattie Shakespeare (8)	91
Ben Faulkner (9)	92
Francesca Gorrill (9)	93
Ethan Southam (8)	94
Jasper Dewulf (8)	95
Cameron Barritt (9)	96
Dylan Coakes (9)	97
Millie May Polito (9)	98
Hunter Le (9)	99
Daniel Beaugrand (9)	100
Esmee-Lily Marchi (9)	101
Peaches Cooper (9)	102
Emily Tutt (9)	103
Cody Meierdirk (8)	104
Tilly Rose-Carless (9)	105
Alex Baskott (8)	106

Damian Bird (8)	107
Dylan Shaw (8)	108
Ben Smart (8)	109
George Rees (9)	110
Rory Grant (9)	111
Max Dehlendorf (9)	112
Oscar Williams (9)	113

St Andrew's Prep, Eastbourne

Jason Roh (10)	114
Charlotte Millar (9)	115
Beatrice Porter (10)	116
Teo DiPasquo (9)	117
Darcie Walton (10)	118
Thomas Price (10)	119
Joe Cornford (10)	120
Charlie Walter (9)	121
Seb Temple (10)	122
Saskia Elliott (9)	123
Kiana Williams (10)	124

St Margaret's CE Primary School, Hollinwood

Sharon Osindero (9)	125
Pola Piotrowska (9)	126
Mabel Conteh (10)	127
Joe Duggan (9)	128
Yousaf (9)	129
Maheen (9)	130
Aaminah (8)	131
Corey Dodman (9)	132
Darcy (9)	133
Rayyan C Malik (9)	134
Ryan (9)	135
Charlie Whalen (10)	136
Lacey (10)	137
Huzdifah (10)	138
Sienna Tucker (10)	139
Joanna Osindero (9)	140
Deen (10)	141
Varun (9)	142
Antonia (10)	143

Maya Pedley (9)	144
Lulya Tewelde (9)	145
Divine (9)	146
Muhammad Asfaan Rafi (8)	147

St Martin's Preparatory School, Grimsby

Matilda Davey (8)	148
Otto Gabriel Johnson (7)	149
Reeva Raghwani (8)	150
Mollie Simmons (8)	151
Spencer Stead (8)	152
Aaria Bhullar (7)	154
Emilie-Grace Roe (8)	155
Noah Kolomashin (8)	156
Nikolaos Oplopoiadis (8)	157
Elliott Wright (8)	158
Rosie Blake (8)	159
Marley Dunham (8)	160

St Mary's Catholic Primary School, Salterbeck

Isabella Welfare (10)	161
Mila Taylor-Kennedy (10)	162
Amelia Briley (9)	163
Danny Hilferty (10)	164
Mylee Weston (10)	166
Amira-Lily Plater (10)	167
Sonny Adams (10)	168
Kye Metherell (10)	169
Oliver Carruthers (10)	170
Gracie Nugent (10)	171
Layla Agnew (10)	172
Amelia Dunleavy (10)	173
Kenzie Sibbald (10)	174
Courtney Hefford (10)	175
Tilly Scott (10)	176
Summer Dummigan (9)	177
Luke McAllister (10)	178
Raine Sharpe (10)	179
Liam Dryden (10)	180

St Wilfrid's Catholic Primary School, Hartford

Brendan Brown (10)	181
Mark Thompson (9)	182
Sarah Baylis (10)	183
Oscar Rowling (10)	184
Taylor Hughes (10)	186
Kornelia Ciborowski (10)	187
Tiarna Murphy (10)	188
Aidan Broady (10)	189
Krzysztof Nathan Kamranczyk (9)	190
Jacob Appleton (10)	191
Lilly Whiston (10)	192
Anna Leavy (10)	193
Sophia Zeta (10)	194
Tess Lucas (10)	195
Mason-Adam Brown (10)	196
Gabriella Proctor (10)	197
Ben Watts (10)	198
Alisha Tomlinson (10)	199
Sayanthana S (10)	200
Bradley Tomlinson (10)	201
Jessica Leigh (9)	202
Ava Child (10)	203
Esme Strong (10)	204
Aimey Kiran (10)	205
Thomas Burston (10)	206
Ethan Coot (10)	207
Layla Barlow (10)	208
Oliver Ho (10)	209
Marshall Meenan (10)	210

Townhill Junior School, Townhill Park

Sienna Goldsack (8)	211
Ivy Salmon (10)	212
Jasmine Allen (9)	214
Jessica Howard (9) & Sofia	215
Orla Salmon (9)	216

Ysgol Gymraeg Y Fenni, Abergavenny

Elan Evans (9)	217
Noni Pook (10)	218
Maddison Edwards (10)	219
Marisa Santiago (11)	220
Rhonwen Croft (9)	221
Izzy Williams (11)	222
Elis Dickenson (10)	223
Maisie Strong (10)	224
Celt Thomas (9)	225
Evie Hollister (10)	226
Eira Lewis (10)	227
Phoebe Evans (9)	228
Lucy Charrington (10)	229
Flo Park (11)	230
Rhoswen Jones (9)	231
Kayla Gerhardt (9)	232

THE POEMS

Romans And Celts

A diamante poem

Romans
Organised, aware
Ruling, conquering, attacking
Caesar, spear, Queen Boudicca, sword
Hunting, conquering, defending
Vicious, defensive
Celts.

Zara Finlay (8)
Clifton Hall School, Newbridge

Light And Darkness

A diamante poem

Darkness
Mischievous, eerie
Creeping, hurting, misleading
Hiding objects, giving happiness
Helping, comforting, shining
Warm, gleaming
Light.

Thomas Adams (8)
Clifton Hall School, Newbridge

Harry And Voldemort

A diamante poem

Harry
Kind, courageous
Saving, fighting, helping
Cares for people, is mean to people
Hunting, attacking, hurting
Horrible, evil
Voldemort.

Sophia Duffie (8)
Clifton Hall School, Newbridge

Summer And Winter

A diamante poem

Summer
Joyful, warm
Playing, swimming, splashing
Diving in the sea, throwing snowballs
Decorating, wrapping, shining
Icy, dreamy
Winter.

Rose Bertile (9)
Clifton Hall School, Newbridge

Mining

A diamante poem

Diamond
Blue, beautiful
Mine, jewel, stone
Shining, sparkling, hypnotising, glistening
Cart, jewellery, robber
Expensive, heavy
Gold.

Rose Butlin (9)
Clifton Hall School, Newbridge

Spring And Winter

A diamante poem

Spring
Beautiful, fun
Growing, enjoying, playing
Flowers, Easter, Santa, hot chocolate
Sledging, giving, opening
Joyful, warm
Winter.

Cara Woolley (8)
Clifton Hall School, Newbridge

Matilda And Miss Trunchbull

A diamante poem

Matilda
Smart, nice
Reading, talking, learning
Books, homework, axe, children
Shaking, throwing, shouting
Mean, big
Miss Trunchbull.

Emily McKay (8)
Clifton Hall School, Newbridge

Unicorns And Horses

A diamante poem

Unicorns
Sparkly, elegant
Flying, walking, running
Rainbows, stables, farms, clouds
Galloping, leaping, jumping
Silky, happy
Horses.

Farrah Youssef (8)
Clifton Hall School, Newbridge

Mythical And Real

A diamante poem

Dragon
Powerful, fierce
Flying, breathing, fighting
Fire, wings, tail, teeth
Climbing, running, roaring
Majestic, sneaky
Panther.

Austin Gunn (8)
Clifton Hall School, Newbridge

Sun And Rain

A diamante poem

Sun
Sunlight, busy
Swimming, growing, playing
Ice cream, beach, umbrella, jacket
Splashing, watering, pouring
Watery, cold
Rain.

Varshika Ganapathiran Sivakamini (8)
Clifton Hall School, Newbridge

Cats And Dogs

A diamante poem

Cats
Cute, furry
Pouncing, eating, meowing
Whiskers, tails, treats, leashes
Growling, running, sleeping
Treats, leashes
Dogs.

Cole Thomson (8)
Clifton Hall School, Newbridge

Night And Day

A diamante poem

Night
Dark, quiet
Sleeping, dreaming, resting
Moon, stars, noise, sunlight
Playing, moving, working
Busy, crowded
Day.

Cameron McKeown (9)
Clifton Hall School, Newbridge

Lonely Moon

A diamante poem

Sun
Bright, beautiful
Flaring, blaring, burning
Day, stars, space, night
Resting, dreaming, sleeping
Quiet, cold
Moon.

Solomon Bisi-Olaitan (8)
Clifton Hall School, Newbridge

Day And Night

A diamante poem

Night,
Quiet, dark
Resting, dreaming, hunting
Stars, moon, sun, cloud
Working, moving, playing
Busy, crowded
Day.

Stephen Hodgson (8)
Clifton Hall School, Newbridge

The Sun And Moon

A diamante poem

Sun
Bright, warm
Flaming, working, burning
Day, stars, space, night
Shining, dreaming, sleeping
Dark, quiet
Moon.

Jamie Kadzimu (8)
Clifton Hall School, Newbridge

Summer And Winter

A diamante poem

Summer
Hot, warm
Swimming, running, playing
Flowers, sun, ice, snow
Sledging, cooling, playing
Cold, icy
Winter.

Noah Dryburgh-Cook (8)
Clifton Hall School, Newbridge

Night And Day

A diamante poem

Night
Dark, quiet
Resting, hunting, dreaming
Star, moon, sun, trees
Playing, working, moving
Busy, noisy
Day.

Ryan Timmins (8)
Clifton Hall School, Newbridge

Summer And Winter

A diamante poem

Winter
Ice, frost
Freezing, chilly
Shivering, shaking, biting
Barbecue, sun
Bright, warm
Summer.

Elspeth Stewart (8)
Clifton Hall School, Newbridge

The Great Christmas Day!

C heering that Christmas has finally come,
H ope to get presents under the special Christmas tree,
R ed ribbons and decorations discovered all around the tall, green, lit-up tree,
I t's totally the best day I can see,
S now starts falling from the ocean-blue sky and everyone runs outside,
T ime flies by and Santa's already here delivering presents,
M ilk and cookies left just for him,
A n amazing day has just begun,
S anta's mission is finally accomplished for this year...

D elivering presents to people,
A day you can't forget,
Y ummy Christmas food getting settled on the table. Time to dig in!

Emilija Stepanova (9)
Downfield Primary School, Cheshunt

Acrobatics

A crobatics is like gymnastics but better!
C ould anything be better?
R ealistically, acrobatics is exercise too.
O bviously, it takes practice to be able to do tricks.
B ackbends are difficult but if you stretch it will be easy.
A mazing, awesome, acrobatics, better than gymnastics.
T rue as Mayo, acrobatics is the right way to go.
I love acrobatics so much.
C lassy, calm and cheerful. Acrobatics is hard but fun,
S urely you will give it a go.

Lauma Pilka (10)
Downfield Primary School, Cheshunt

Different Things

If you are playing soccer and you hit the crossbar,
A teammate will sing *la, la, la.*
When playing Mario, control Donkey Kong,
If you win, whisper 'Shing Shong!'
Jesus created Easter,
Christians want a computer!
Buy a Lamborghini,
Then find a person called Greeny.
If you do maths revision,
You will do division.
If you mutter,
You're a nutter.
If you play soccer and you're a CAM,
For dinner, you eat lamb.
Then rhyme
And sing along to a chime!

Joseph Morrison (10)
Downfield Primary School, Cheshunt

Gymnastics

Gymnastics is important to me,
An Olympian is something I want to be.
I work hard every day,
So I can learn the coach's way.
On vault I run and jump.
I only hope my head doesn't bump.
On bars you see me swing and cast
As I zip around very fast.
Balance is important on the beam,
Dancing on the floor it may seem.
With grace you'll see me dance and flip,
My floor routine is such a trip!
An Olympian is something I want to be,
Gymnastics is important to me!

Sophie Butcher (9)
Downfield Primary School, Cheshunt

Nature Is...

Nature is calm, peaceful and quiet,
Loud, fast and destructive.
When it is angry it can growl like a lion.
Nature is hot, smoky and burning,
Clear, wet and flowing.
Its clear liquid can spread life and can grow forests.
Nature is red, green and blue,
Yellow, brown and grey.
If you look closer all the colours are there.
Nature is bright, colourful and alive,
Swampy, polluted and dying.
Though it is beautiful,
It still needs our help.

Emily Lugg (10)
Downfield Primary School, Cheshunt

My Hamster

M y hamster is called Honey
Y ou can pet her and feed her, she'll give you love

H oney loves to eat and play
A ctive at night and asleep in the day
M any hours of fun with her
S itting in her food bowl she nibbles her treats
T rying new snacks she loves to eat
E very 7pm she comes out to play
R unning wild on her neon green wheel.

I love my hamster and she loves me too.

Talulah Sambrook (10)
Downfield Primary School, Cheshunt

The Fight

Sometimes you have a light fight,
So you really need someone to talk.
Since you were actually so upset,
You go outside and have a walk.

They can be kind of mean to you
And get a little aggressive.
You get really scared,
So you then try to be unexpressive.

Now you're really tired of the fight
And you can barely sleep hours.
Asking yourself when will it stop.
Then on your bed you see a bouquet of flowers.

Elif Demikiran (10)
Downfield Primary School, Cheshunt

Summertime

- **S** lurping slushies in the sun
- **U** sing umbrellas to block the heat
- **M** aking sandcastles from the bright yellow sand
- **M** elting ice cream dripping down my hand
- **E** xploring new areas
- **R** iding my bike in the park
- **T** rips and flights being booked
- **I** ce lollies disappearing from the fridge
- **M** assive water balloon fights in the garden
- **E** asy days full of fun.

Zoe Ma (9)
Downfield Primary School, Cheshunt

Halloween

As the moon rises into the night sky,
Bats start to fly.
Children dressed in costumes roam the empty streets,
Collecting sweets from people they meet.
The silver eye watches down from above
And see people not caring about doves.
Decorations cover the houses
And you can no longer see playhouses.
But in the end they all go to sleep
And in their head they're counting sheep.

Maia Gustavsson (10)
Downfield Primary School, Cheshunt

Swimming

S wirling and twirling, dancing and prancing
W inning and losing never makes me sad
I love swimming, it makes me happy
M any other sports but I pick swimming
M onsters and the Loch Ness monster can never stop me from swimming
I n bed I never stop thinking about it
N ever ever will I stop my passion
G oing and never stopping.

Rogue Jacks (10)
Downfield Primary School, Cheshunt

Nature

N othing compares to our wondrous world,
A ll seasons are beautiful and unique,
T all, towering trees and glowing green grass are home to animals we don't see,
U nder the sun, under the moon, life is never asleep,
R unning wild and roaming free,
E normous creatures to miniature bugs, we all need each other.

Florence Smith (10)
Downfield Primary School, Cheshunt

Lionel Messi, The GOAT

Ru **L** ing the world of football.
    I gnites our excitement.
    O n the ball.
    N ever misses.
    E ra of greatness.
    L egend of Argentina.

    M agical scorer.
    E clipsing Ronaldo.
    S hining over the net.
    S uper striker.
    I rreplaceable from the football world.

Charlie Knipes (9)
Downfield Primary School, Cheshunt

Flowers In Bloom

Flowers are bright, flowers are colourful.
They love to be under the sun.
In the garden, at the park,
In the shops, at your house,
They really love to be anywhere.
When they are ready they bloom,
Ready for all the bumblebees.
Flowers are bright, flowers are colourful,
Everyone loves a good old flower.

Chloe Bennett (10)
Downfield Primary School, Cheshunt

Burgers

B ursting with flavour.
U nusual but surprisingly pleasant.
R umbling tummies wish for it.
G reat foods cannot compare to this.
E very part of the burger is made to perfection.
R avishing, yet to be eaten with our hands.
S auce sticking on your fingers.

Sienna Edwards (10)
Downfield Primary School, Cheshunt

Harry

Yo, my name is H,
That's short for Harry.
I play for a rugby team
Which they say I carry.
I score tries quicker
Than I can flick flies.
They say I'm unstoppable
But that's not possible
Because if you tie my laces together
I would look like a fool altogether.

Harry Bennett (10)
Downfield Primary School, Cheshunt

A Dog's Tail

Big paws, small paws,
All different-shaped paws!

All dogs are lovely,
In their different breeds!

Small dogs, tall dogs,
All different-sized dogs,
With their cute floppy ears
And their wet shiny noses!

They give the best cuddles
Like nobody knows!

Lucy Roe (10)
Downfield Primary School, Cheshunt

The Land Above

In a land of beauty so divine,
Where crystal waters gently shine,
The sun sets in a golden hue
And skies of blue are always true,
The so-soft sand beneath your feet,
The ocean breeze so sweet and neat,
A paradise for all to see,
This earthly heaven, forever free.

Diego Sacko (10)
Downfield Primary School, Cheshunt

The Roman Empire

R omans lived in a massive Empire.
O wned land in Europe, Africa and Asia.
M asters at conquering.
A n empire that lasted over 1,000 years.
N ow it doesn't exist anymore.
S o we don't need to worry about the Empire.

Eron Xhemshiti (10)
Downfield Primary School, Cheshunt

The Killer

L ions tasty prey
E xcellent at pouncing
O n the tree for the big jump
P reciously looking after their babies
A lways on their big night hunt
R unning wild
D ead is where you now belong.

Yuina Honda (10)
Downfield Primary School, Cheshunt

Cheese

C heesily good.
H appily grated or sliced.
E asily tasty.
E xtra for everything.
S omething I like to eat.
E veryday meal.

Riley Phillips (10)
Downfield Primary School, Cheshunt

The Snake

Snake, snake all you do is slither around,
Yes, all you do is slither around but not around the town.
Dost thou think o'er what they have done?
No you don't because you're benighted like a bat.
Slithery, benighted snake, you're always in your cave.
Slithery snake when animals are around you're brave.
Dost thou think that you are brave?
Or inside the emmet are you just afraid?
Snake, you're sly, all the movement you do is slither,
You're sly and rude, snake you're a wither.
I thought thou were thy friend,
No snake, because you're bewitched.
Scaly snake slither down, you act like a child,
Dost thou think o'er what they do?
Snake, snake all you do is slither around,
Yes, all you do is slither but not around town.

Aria Holland (10)
Etching Hill Primary School, Etching Hill

The Cat

Cat, cat sitting in a round, itchy, uncomfortable hat,
I gaze at thou scratching my old mat,
Always chasing invading mice, like a tiger in the night,
How are thou not afraid when thou jumps from a height?

Living in my small, cosy, humble home,
Thou seem to hate my gnome,
Making a home in a cardboard box,
Dost thou know I bought a bed for a reason?

Your paws make me smile,
Your claws make my heart beat faster than when I ran a mile,
Your fur looks as soft as a bed,
Even though you clean yourself with saliva.

Dost thou know thou walks so careful and gentle?
Even though thou jumps a bit mental,
I know thou always lands on your feet,
But sometimes thou has your moment of defeat!

Thou jumps at poor, innocent, feathery birds
And get loads of delight if thy come in herds,
Thou curl up and get some rest,
After thou attacked a bird's nest.

Cat, cat sitting in a round, itchy, uncomfortable hat,
I gaze at thou scratching my old mat,
Always chasing invading mice, like a tiger in the night,
How are thou not afraid when thou jumps from a height?

Amber Laud (10)
Etching Hill Primary School, Etching Hill

The Fox!

Fox, fox in the woods,
Always in the dark looking for prey,
Trying to find a way.
It scrambles and searches for great prey
And when it finds its prey
It happily cheers hooray!

Chilling in thy forest,
Sleeping in thy forest,
If thou goes in the dark
Thou will see a homely forest,
Why are you so sly
And so very benighted?

The sly orange fox is so sneaky,
It could pick twelve locks.
At night it whines in the dark,
As its tail swishes any glimmers in the moonlight.
If thou see thy fox, it will be sneaking,
Hiding in thy grass, it will be peeking.

Will thou have the honour to see its fiery fur?
Thy fox's tail swishes in the wind.
The fearful fox ready to fight,
Thy fearful fox is ready to bite.
You're looking for its prey.
The strong fox sneaks around.

Fox, fox in the woods,
Always in the dark looking for prey,
Trying to find a way.
It scrambles and searches for great prey
And when it finds its prey
It happily cheers hooray!

Virginia Maduakor (10)
Etching Hill Primary School, Etching Hill

The Rabbit

Rabbit, rabbit, why dost thou hide?
Is it fear, or too little pride?
You jump and leap through the night,
To spot a fox must cause thee fright!

Why dost thou dig a home underground?
Is it to avoid them as you are so renowned?
In the forest, your tangles, sprays of ivy climb,
The burrow homes and carrots thou found,
Are they good enough to create a bind?

Why dost thou have such long ears?
Is it to help thou hear?
Thou tail - small yet soft,
Thou teeth - large and strong!

Why dost thou leap over such a log,
Thou is like a robot who lost a cog!
Leaping, jumping, bouncing, hopping!
Why dost thou have such energy?

Why dost thou never seem outworn?
Why dost thou never seem forlorn?
Bouncing but hiding,
Burrowing but never climbing!
You run and hop until you drop!

Rabbit, rabbit, why dost thou hide?
Is it fear, or too little pride?
You jump and leap through the night,
To spot a fox must cause thee fright!

Chloe Bateman (10)
Etching Hill Primary School, Etching Hill

The Duck

Duck, you're so cute and nice,
Your favourite food is rice.
Thou have a bright yellow glow
And in the pond you're racing away.

In what distant deep or skies
Could burn the fire of those fine eyes.
Why dost you hide at night
But play in the deep dark forest?

And what should and what could
Twist the string of the heart?
You're so small, as small as my hand
But sometimes you're so clueless.

Thou wobble all day and night
And all the time you're so bright.
When I put music on you're dancing and prancing
And when there's food your crunching and munching.

You're a cheetah when predators are seeking,
But why dost you be peeking,
You're a cute, fluffy duck,
When you play trees are waving

Duck, duck, you're so cute and nice,
Your favourite food is rice.
Thou have a bright yellow glow
And in the pond you're racing away.

Connor Stevenson (10)
Etching Hill Primary School, Etching Hill

The Snake

Snake, snake you're everyone's foe,
Why are thou on the earth so low?
No one can have a glance at thou,
He's dangerous and deadly to you, can stretch,
Really high, I told you now!

Living in thy wide land so dry,
People think, *you can't survive when the clouds don't cry!*
Well, you proved thee wrong,
Oh, we are very wrong.

Why dost thou have rough, tough, leathery skin?
Why dost thou shed and leave a skin so thin?
And because you are an emerald-green,
Be careful you are not seen!

Slithering through thy hammering rain,
The faster thou goes, the more speed thou gains!
He catches his prey, so delicious,
But the way thee does it is so vicious.

How dost thou have venom in thy mouth?
Why dost it kill them?
Why is thee so harsh and tough?
With everything thou dost thee have to be rough!

Victoria Sopron (10)
Etching Hill Primary School, Etching Hill

The Lion

Lion, lion always growling,
Around the dark you're always prowling,
Day and night you're always stalking,
Unseen and fearless and brave.

In the scorching savannah,
When clouds are light,
Darkness fills you, this is where you lie,
At night silence is all you hear,
Making it mysterious and distant.

In the night why dost it be so bright?
But will it ever bite?
So elegant and versatile
Your fluffy mane is so soft.

Dazzling, sprinting, sneaking,
Never ever stop creeping.
Walking proudly,
Roaring so loudly.

In the day you always bite,
In the night you're always bright.
Your big teeth are always at work
And you never stop to think.

Lion, lion always growling,
Around the dark you're always prowling,
Day and night you're always stalking,
Unseen and fearless and brave.

Oscar Harwood (10)
Etching Hill Primary School, Etching Hill

Shark, Shark

Shark, shark in the Atlantic,
Always manic.
Surfs for its prey,
Never is okay.

Shark, shark, attacks its prey,
Thou might find this creature in the ocean.
Don't worry, it doesn't take potions.
Thou will find it sleeping,
You make a noise you'll see it peering.

The dangerous, feisty shark
Will give you a nice bite.
Don't go near it
Or else say night-night.

This creature is sneaky,
So don't be cheeky.
It is spying and shy,
If you see it coming prepare to die.

Thy creature has a small nose
But it does not pose,
O'er its shiny, slimy fearless fin,
Even though it's as sharp as a pin.

Shark, shark see it in the Atlantic,
Always manic.
Surfs for its prey,
Never is okay.
Shark, shark attacks its prey.

Daniel Liddle (10)
Etching Hill Primary School, Etching Hill

The Turkey

Turkey, turkey standing small,
Who would ever eat thou at all?
Oh what wings dare thou aspire?
What hand dare seize thy fire?

Tiny turkey sneaking all day,
Until when Christmas comes he gets taken away.
In the farm thou are sneaking,
At night thou foe is speaking.

With a long pointy beak,
It shall thou peek.
As tiny as a dot,
You still use it to eat a lot.

While walking slowly,
When you walk you're always lonely.
You're so small,
So all the animals are so tall.

Loud turkey gobbling and gobbling,
Until at night-time thou starts wobbling,
But droop thou tender wing
And forget thou youthful spring.

Turkey, turkey standing small,
Who would ever eat thou at all?
On what wings dare thou aspire?
What hand dare seize thy fire?

Freya Vukmirovic (10)
Etching Hill Primary School, Etching Hill

Cheetah

Cheetah, cheetah likes to run
But in seconds they'll be done.
Like a human they love to hunt,
They work so hard, they're never dumb.

In the winds of Africa they are gliding,
But in the bush they will be hiding.
Their dark coat is always shining,
Have thou ever seen it flying?

If thou sees it coming,
Don't stop running,
Leaping, hiking, hitting,
It never stops.

If thou sees it spying,
Dost not start flying,
O'er the morning noon,
Thou might end up in doom.

Thou see it creeping,
At night shines bright while sleeping,
Like a knight in shining armour,
But likes a bit of drama.

Cheetah, cheetah likes to run,
But in seconds they'll be done.

Rosie Jackson (10)
Etching Hill Primary School, Etching Hill

The Snake

Snake, snake sneak around thy day,
Then go home when it's down,
And sleep till another day,
Where dost thy go?

Thy is the controller,
Thy is the patroller
Of thy grass,
Where's thy grass?

With some dark green scales,
That goes through a field of spikes
And thy's white fangs
And thy's small black eyes.

Thy slithering around
Until thy goes out of bounds,
Thy slithers until thy's benighted,
Why does thy sun go down?

Thy may hiss,
Thy may spit,
But thy never backs away.
Why do thy never back away?

Snake, snake sneak around the day,
Then go home when it's down
And sleep till another day.
Where dost thy go?

Isobel S-B (10)
Etching Hill Primary School, Etching Hill

The Cheetah

Cheetah, cheetah running fast,
Could thou dost this in the past?
What else can thou do?

Deep into the forest, thou is biting,
I wonder what thou is doing, are thou fighting?
Can thou hear the voice?
Thou hear the voice, thou rejoice!

Trying to be top,
Looking like gold,
Oh how thou ears fold,
Also looking bold.

As thou is creeping,
Birds are creeping,
Suddenly, thou pounce!
Biting, killing, slowly tearing...

Pitying thou dropped a tear,
But thou saw a glowworm near,
Who replied, "What wailing white?"
Calls the watchman of the night.

Cheetah, cheetah running fast,
Could thou dost this in the past?
What else can thou dost?

Georgia Bott (10)
Etching Hill Primary School, Etching Hill

The Snake

Snake, snake, hiding and peeking,
In the grass always sneaking.
In the jungle of the night,
Who will ever come across you at night?

If thy is slithering and racing outdoors
You are chasing through the jungle,
Thou will see them at thy jungle.

In the jungle thou are creeping
You are creeping as you are green
Be careful you're not seen
Dost thou know who made thee?

In the morning thou are fighting
But then you're biting.
You swerve and glide with such pride,
Dost thou know who made thee?

Hiding and peeking,
In the grass always sneaking.
In the jungle of the night,
Who will come across you at night?

Alexia Wharton (10)
Etching Hill Primary School, Etching Hill

The Bat

Bat, bat always flying,
Catching bugs and sneakily spying,
When thou hides during the morning is thou sleeping
Or is thou weeping?

Why dost you keep inside
When it is bright?
And why come out when thou colony is asleep?
Dost you dare move?

When you're swooping through the trees
Does thou get time for sneezing?
When you return to the dark
How does thou sleep?

As thou is gliding
Does thou feel like hiding?
For the size of thou is so small.

Bat, bat always flying,
Catching bugs and sneakily spying,
When you hide during the morning
Is thou sleeping or is thou weeping?

Emilia Halberda (10)
Etching Hill Primary School, Etching Hill

If I Ruled The World...

If I ruled the world I'd like to help the poor,
Give them shelter, give them food, just make sure they had more.
If I ruled the world I'd like to make it fair,
No more greed and excess wealth, everyone would share.
If I ruled the world I'd make sure all war ends,
Stop all fighting everywhere - we could just be friends.
If I ruled the world I'd look after Planet Earth,
Plant more trees, burn less fuels, give it a whole rebirth.
If I ruled the world I'd like to make it better,
Free clothes for everyone - maybe a bright pink sweater.
If I ruled the world I wouldn't go to school,
But then again, I need to learn or I'd end up being a fool.
If I ruled the world I'd like to learn to fly,
I'd put on my cape and mask and leap into the sky.
If I ruled the world it would be a better place,
Lit up by the beaming smile on my little face.

Imogen Mills (10)
Haughton St Giles CE Primary Academy, Haughton

My Garden

M y family and I love being in our garden
Y ou will always find me and my sister jumping as high as a gazelle on our trampoline

G rowing vegetables for us to eat, tasty tomatoes, curly kale and runner beans climbing high
A nts, snails and bugs my little brother loves to find
R ays of sunshine shine down from the sky
D ad mows the lawn while Mum makes a lovely lunch
E verybody excitedly listening for the ice cream man to arrive
N esting birds fly down from the tree, hoping to find crumbs we left from our tea.

Esmee Whittingham (8)
Haughton St Giles CE Primary Academy, Haughton

The Hungry Dragon Who Ate Our School

The day the dragon came to call,
She smashed the gate and ate the wall,
She ate and ate the entrance hall,
The staffroom table, teachers and all
And began to chase a basketball.

So...
She's undeniably great,
She's absolutely cool,
The dragon who ate,
The dragon who ate,
The dragon who ate our school.

Pupils brawled, teachers ran,
She flew at them with a great big bam,
She slew a few women and a man
And chewed through an ice cream van,
Then crashed into a big fat man.

Victoria Kolasa (9)
Haughton St Giles CE Primary Academy, Haughton

The Joyful Daffodil

This daffodil is extremely happy,
When it bobs its head at people walking by.

She whistles a heart-warming tune
When people start to cry.

She makes people's day by politely smiling
And dancing in the breeze.

She has a vibrant green stem that glows in the night sky,
She has a bright yellow scintillating flower head that shines in the sunlight.

She has so many friends she can't choose the best one,
This sweet and loving daffodil is inspiring.

Marley Hague (9)
Haughton St Giles CE Primary Academy, Haughton

The Day The Dragon Came To Call

The day the dragon came to call,
He bit the classroom wall,
The teacher came to stall,
The dragon came to haul,
The dragon ate my basketball.

Now...
She's undeniably great,
She's absolutely cool,
The dragon who ate,
The dragon who ate,
The dragon who ate our school.

Everyone screamed,
Teachers fell in the dragon's drool,
He came and fell, the class pet, Paul
And now pupils want to crawl.

Phoebe Widger (10)
Haughton St Giles CE Primary Academy, Haughton

Love Brew

Get mushrooms with the sparkliest touch,
To glimmer your eyes,
On the floor with misty dust,
Blow dandelions to spread the nature touch,
Mush poppies for a red paint spread,
Grow trees
For our amazing bees,
The bird of paradise looks over our loving world,
Orchids blossom,
Water lilies bop happily on the long rivers whilst love brings
Tulips sing along with a joyful tune.

Boris Hubev (8)
Haughton St Giles CE Primary Academy, Haughton

My Hobbies

I have lots of hobbies,
Like horse riding and gymnastics.
They're really fun, you should give one a try.
I like my hobbies,
They put me in a good mood,
Hard or easy, I'll do it any time of the day.
Break a bone, fall off,
I'll never give up.
When I'm scared I will tell,
I never give up.

Eva Lamont (8)
Haughton St Giles CE Primary Academy, Haughton

Who Am I?

I play for PSG.
The number on my shirt is 30.
I played against Ronaldo.
My best mates are Mbappé and Neymar.
I scored some goals against Ronaldo.
I played in the World Cup with Argentina and won it.
I have played a lot of games.
I am the GOAT of all time.
Who am I?

Answer: Messi.

Davie Willmott (9)
Haughton St Giles CE Primary Academy, Haughton

What Am I?

I am fierce,
I am scary,
I am strong,
I fly over the sea for food,
I have three heads,
I am green,
Every day I fly over a castle,
When I am flying I see a girl called Bella,
She lives in a brown castle,
She sometimes waves at me, so I wave back.
Do you know what I am?
I am a mega monster.

Jayden Edwards (8)
Haughton St Giles CE Primary Academy, Haughton

This Is Me

T ap dancing is my favourite dance
H orse riding is my favourite hobby
I love my friends and family
S ometimes I make mistakes

I love the author David Walliams
S tronger than I look

M e, I know I am unique
E verything I love is nature and us.

Layla Brain (8)
Haughton St Giles CE Primary Academy, Haughton

All About Me!

I love my dog Lilly,
Although she is sometimes silly,
My friends and family are the best,
They are so nice I feel blessed,
School is great,
But maths, makes my brain ache,
I also love acting,
Since it has lots of interacting,
Gymnastics is my pleasure
And I'll never give it up for treasure.

Izabela Hubeva (10)
Haughton St Giles CE Primary Academy, Haughton

Plants

Plants are green
And in the sun
They gleam
Like a sparkle.

Their petals
Come in lots of shades,
They sometimes look like
The colour of jade.

Their leaves
Have lots of types of lines
For their veins
But sometimes they have vines!

Seren Abell (8)
Haughton St Giles CE Primary Academy, Haughton

Football

F ootball is my favourite sport
O range is the half-time snack
O h I love to play football
T he teams are cheering
B ut I hate when they score
A lways a penalty
L ove to score
L ove to play.

Grace Wardell (11)
Haughton St Giles CE Primary Academy, Haughton

The Best Dream

When I went to sleep I had the best dream.
I was a tiger
Chasing and killing people
Until I was brought to a shelter.
Everyone saw me
And they laughed
Until my alarm woke me up.

George Gardiner (8)
Haughton St Giles CE Primary Academy, Haughton

Friends For Life

Friends come and go,
But true friends stay.

I have lots of friends
That I'm glad to have.

I have my friends
I know
We will be
Friends forever!

Emelia Allen (11)
Haughton St Giles CE Primary Academy, Haughton

Black Cats

Black cats marching in,
Through the dark and through the dim.
Scratch, scratch, paw, paw,
Mice beware of their deadly claws.
Crouching down, pouncing at birds,
But still too quiet to be heard.
With fur like midnight, eyes like the moon,
They can lead some animals to their doom.
When they're on the streets,
They'll give a deafening yowl,
So frightening, you would want to hide under a towel.
Now you know the black cat's secret,
Don't let their revenge be on you!
You, that will never call a black cat cute.

Lily Parnell (9)
Inkberrow Primary School, Inkberrow

The Holiday

Over in Florida where the sun always shines,
Lives a big friendly mouse who comes to meet you at times.

The rides are amazing, they tumble you around,
But while you are here, you will spend more than a pound!

The food is delicious, the ice cream is for me,
Along with pancakes that are shaped like Mickey.

The best holiday ever I will never forget,
Just watch out for rainclouds, they will get you wet.

Have you guessed where I am yet?
It is the best place to be,
The one and only...
Walt Disney!

Isla Taylor (9)
Inkberrow Primary School, Inkberrow

Cloud Shapes

Clouds go by,
Way up high,
Dinosaur, pig, I love it all,
Many shapes rise and fall.

Lying in the sun,
Having fun,
Imagination running wild,
The clouds are smiling like a child.

Squirrel, monkey running around,
The wind is blowing but makes no sound,
The tickly grass against my back,
It's getting late, I need a snack!

Clouds like oceans of white,
What a pretty sight!
Nature's art so good to see,
Why don't you join me?

Florence White (9)
Inkberrow Primary School, Inkberrow

Love

L ove is wild and magical. Love is great, it's a thing no one can hate.
O ne is a number, two is great, three is love that is greater than great.
V icious is bad and so are you, so instead spread love around this zoo.
E lephants are loving and cute too, so you can't disappoint when they look at you.

Olivia Seal (9)
Inkberrow Primary School, Inkberrow

The Horror Of Vegetables

I look on my plate and get a shock,
This mushy horror isn't chips,
Or chicken nuggets, burgers either,
There are no tacos or ketchup dip!

Instead I see an emerald horror,
Cabbage like a lumpy towel,
Celery that spikes my mouth
And digs in my stomach like a gardening trowel.

"Eat your vegetables!" says Mum,
I could only stare with wide eyes,
What I thought was to be a lovely dinner,
Turned out to be a disgusting surprise!

Sure, they say carrots can make you see in the dark,
But that's just to make you hunch
Over your disgusting vegetables,
They say that to make you eat your lunch.

So when your mum asks, "What do you want to eat?"
Make sure you make it crystal clear,
That you don't, don't, don't want vegetables,
Once you say that, have no fear!

And if your dearest mother gets cross,
If she says, "Miss, you're getting edgy!"
Then you say, "I'm sorry, Mum,
I just don't want to eat my veggies."

Eileen Chapman (9)
Lancing Prep At Worthing, Worthing

Pizza!

I joyfully walk into a pizza shop,
The smell is just divine!
I look over at a pizza, it smiled,
I knew it must be mine.

The smell is quite delicious,
It's even a bit pineappley,
I want to just go...
Yum, yum, yummy!
Put it all into my tummy!
The smell
It lingers on the nose and mouth,
Tickling you all about.

Peppers are red and sweet,
Spicy pepperoni, my tastebuds set alight
As I slowly take a bite!
Mmmm!
Crispy, crunchy crusts,
Stringy Cheddar cheese, I say,
"Oh my gosh! Can I have another one please?"

Elliott Sandell (9)
Lancing Prep At Worthing, Worthing

Chicken Milanese

C runchy breadcrumbs
H ot, delicious, chewy chicken
I nspirational food in my mouth
C risp and golden light outside
K itchen smells delightful when we cook
E ating it makes me drool for hours
N othing is better!

M unching away on the flaky batter
I imagine eating it in my dream
L ovely soft chicken inside, loads of breadcrumbs
A stounding taste
N ever wasting it
E at every bite
S mells like a fresh chicken out of the oven
E verything gone!

Eithne Wallace Nannig (9)
Lancing Prep At Worthing, Worthing

Noodles For Tea!

My mum asks me, "What do you want for tea?"
I say, "Noodles please!"
As I wait I think of slurping those noodles up with ease.
The dinner lands on the plate.
I'm so excited for this dinner date!
It's on the table, I get my fork
Or maybe my spork?
I wonder what flavour it will be?
Chicken? Plain? Sweet and sour? Or maybe spicy?
I sit at the table,
Mum better not be telling a fable!
She puts the dinner down,
It's definitely not a frown.
On my plate it's sweet and sour,
Oh, it has a lot of power!

Autumn Shore (8)
Lancing Prep At Worthing, Worthing

I Adore Lemon Meringue Tart!

The tangy flavour pierces my taste buds
Like a thousand knives,
The sides crunch like a crumbling brick,
My tongue explodes as I take a lick,
Crunch, crunch.
Its creamy insides burst like a gorilla's punch,
It winds my tongue, tickles my tooth,
It will ruin my youth,
Its sweet smell is a good sign,
The lemon electrocutes me like a power line,
The meringue on the top is like a cloud,
Its juicy scent is very loud,
I adore lemon meringue tart!
Oh, yes I do!

Amalie Subedar (9)
Lancing Prep At Worthing, Worthing

Bubble Tea

B alls in my watering mouth and the sweet juice pours out
U nbelievably yummy in my tummy
B ubbles, bubbles everywhere
B eautiful and tasty too
L et the juice go down into my tummy, mmm!
E ager to get another one!

T ogether the smooth balls swim around
E ating, slurping the juice in one gulp
A juicy, wonderful, yummy bubble tea is so scrumptious. Yum!

Elodie Gibbs (9)
Lancing Prep At Worthing, Worthing

Bubble Tea

B alls in my mouth feeling them pop
U nbelievably, uncontrollably juicy and sweet
B ouncing ice rocking about, clashing into each other
B eautiful, fruity, juicy going up the straw
L uxuriously running down my throat
E xtraordinarily yummy in my tummy

T easing my tastebuds
E ating the balls and slurping the juice
A ddicted to this juicy drink.

Hattie Shakespeare (8)
Lancing Prep At Worthing, Worthing

The Amazing Brownie

B rown as delicious melting chocolate
R ectangular in shape, not my favourite subject
O dd to look at but so yummy to eat
W ell cooked, well done, hard to ignore, have to eat
N ever forget your favourite food. Brownie, brownie, brownie
I cing is the magic touch covering the top
E very brownie is delightful, don't miss this delicious treat!

Ben Faulkner (9)
Lancing Prep At Worthing, Worthing

Ice Cream

I cy tang on a scorching hot day
C reamy fluff topped with a flake
E veryone squeals at the incredible taste

C runchy cone waiting for the drip
R aspberry sorbet, vanilla delight and mint choc chip
E ndless brain freeze from my tongue
A rgh! It's cold!
M elts slowly in the heat, screaming as it gets stolen by a seagull.

Francesca Gorrill (9)
Lancing Prep At Worthing, Worthing

Hot Dogs!

H ot crispy bun
O m, *nom, nom,* it goes down so good, so juicy
T ender in my mouth

D reaming of them
O m, *nom, nom,* it goes down so good, so juicy
G ood, so good in my mouth, the taste sticks
S izzling sausages, sauce spread like a carpet

According to me the best New York food ever!

Ethan Southam (8)
Lancing Prep At Worthing, Worthing

Pizza

Cheesy delight.
Red tomato, deliciously sweet,
Covering my lips and mouth,
Divine crunchy crust.
Remember to order double-crusted pizza!
The smell of spicy, cheese and chicken pizza
Making me dribble like a dog!
The greasy egg yolk
Giving it an extraordinary taste!
When the stringy cheese goes in your mouth
You will want pizza forever.

Jasper Dewulf (8)
Lancing Prep At Worthing, Worthing

Pizza

Peppers red and sweet, spicy pepperoni,
My tastebuds set alight
As I slowly take a bite,
Hot greasy goodness.
Absolutely scrumptious,
It smells of...
Gooey, stringy, oozing cheese,
Bright red, juicy tomatoes,
Sizzling altogether like piping-hot lava,
Fluffy as pillows,
On the inside of the crust,
Pizza is scrumdiddlyumptious!

Cameron Barritt (9)
Lancing Prep At Worthing, Worthing

Mystery Food

I am a food - a bread,
Hard outside, soft inside with a crunchy crust,
Most people think I have a strong smell,
But I think not!
I am as round as a Frisbee,
You would eat me with pasta,
You might have me with cheese on,
I am yummy and scrummy.
You feel free when you eat me,
I am garlic bread,
Come eat me now!

Dylan Coakes (9)
Lancing Prep At Worthing, Worthing

My Glorious Cupcake!

There's nothing more I would eat,
Something sweet and a big treat.
A cupcake!
That's what I need
But I just need one more thing.
Some yummy and colourful...
Sprinkles! Nothing like crunchy rainbow,
Millions of sprinkles,
But when I eat a cupcake I taste...
Sweet and glorious, as smooth as a fluffy pillow.

Millie May Polito (9)
Lancing Prep At Worthing, Worthing

The Secret Ingredient

Sparkles in the sunlight.
Cold as snow.
Eat me and you will feel good.
Different colour choices like the colourful rainbow.
You would want me in the summer
But there is something bad about me,
You get a brain freeze,
Your energy goes hyper.
What am I?

Answer: Ice cream.

Hunter Le (9)
Lancing Prep At Worthing, Worthing

What Am I?

I am as crunchy as bone
But I have a soft inside, as soft as wool.
I am as gold as the sun
And as hot as it too!
I am so thin, I am as thin as paper
Yet I am slightly wide in the shape of a cuboid,
Yet I am as tasty and similarly spelt like crisps.
What am I?

Answer: Chips.

Daniel Beaugrand (9)
Lancing Prep At Worthing, Worthing

Guess The Food

Sticky skin.
Squishy surprise.
Marshmallow, *munch*.
Cornflake, *crunch*.
Chocolate smell up my nose.
Rectangle, round, round the corner.
What do you think I am?
I dissolve in your mouth
And I am really yummy.
What am I?

Answer: Rocky road.

Esmee-Lily Marchi (9)
Lancing Prep At Worthing, Worthing

Crunchy Popcorn

P opping madly in the microwave
O range, cream, yellow, red, loads of colours to choose
P erfect cooking just for me
C runchy as a chewy Twix
O dd in shape but delicious to eat
R emember to bring me when you go to the movies
N ice taste too!

Peaches Cooper (9)
Lancing Prep At Worthing, Worthing

Delicious Doughnuts

D elicious jammy middle
O h I love doughnuts
U nique with shapes and sizes
G reat for picnic days
H eaps of bright icing colours
N utritiously fluffy bread
U nlimited sweetness
T remendously flavourful with all kinds of sauces.

Emily Tutt (9)
Lancing Prep At Worthing, Worthing

Mac 'N' Cheese

Mac 'n' cheese is yummy,
Going to my tummy!
As the cheese melts in your mouth
You think...
Mac 'n' cheese is yummy,
Going to my tummy!
It's deliciously delicious and piping hot,
Don't whack my knees for mac 'n' cheese.

Cody Meierdirk (8)
Lancing Prep At Worthing, Worthing

Sprinkles

I am covered in sprinkles
As colourful as a rainbow.
When you bite into me you'll see my blood.
I look like a deep pit.
I have icing as sweet as a treat.
I have a food in my name but I won't tell you what.
Guess what I am?

Answer: A doughnut.

Tilly Rose-Carless (9)
Lancing Prep At Worthing, Worthing

Super Spaghetti

S lowly eat the outstanding treat
P urely significant
A mazingly tasty
G obble up the fascinating dinner
H eaven is what you eat
E normously filling
T ongue loving
T ummy tickling
I ncredibly yummy.

Alex Baskott (8)
Lancing Prep At Worthing, Worthing

Coke

C ourageously fizzy and bubbles about in your mouth
O utrageously sugary! Sugar galore! It is amazingly scrumptious!
K itchen gets filled with the sugary drink as I resist the temptation.
E legantly goes down your throat as you enter your dreams.

Damian Bird (8)
Lancing Prep At Worthing, Worthing

Apples

- **A** is for all the juiciness
- **P** is for picking the disgusting seeds out
- **P** is for perfect colour, sometimes red, sometimes green
- **L** is for liking the red, not the green
- **E** is for expecting tastiness
- **S** is for super crunchy.

Dylan Shaw (8)
Lancing Prep At Worthing, Worthing

Perfect Pancake

P is for flipping the pan
A is for amazing toppings
N is for nutritiously delicious food
C is for crispy edges
A is for adoringly sweet and juicy
K is for king-sized pancake
E is for an enormous tummy.

Ben Smart (8)
Lancing Prep At Worthing, Worthing

Ice Cream On The Summer Beach

I rresistible to eat
C alling in the summer breeze
E at any time

C reate any flavours
R anges of colours
E xceptionally cold
A delicious treat at the beach
M ight get a brain freeze.

George Rees (9)
Lancing Prep At Worthing, Worthing

Man, I Love Sushi

S esame seeds, *squish, crunch*
U nder my tongue, sticky rice as soft as marshmallows
S alty soy sauce, *chop, chop,* my tastebuds pop
H ealthy, tasty, chewy fish
I say, "Yay sushi, you're so juicy.

Rory Grant (9)
Lancing Prep At Worthing, Worthing

A Morning Treat

T asty flavour
O utstanding texture
A mazing crunch
S pread the delicious sticky jam
T oast is so good.

Max Dehlendorf (9)
Lancing Prep At Worthing, Worthing

Apple

A haiku

It's full of apples,
It's amazing with rhubarb,
It warms up my mouth.

Oscar Williams (9)
Lancing Prep At Worthing, Worthing

Animals

In our world, many animals are being killed by rubbish.
The polar bears' houses are melting.
The animals are creatures too, like us.
We were animals many years ago.

Seals are strangled by rubbish.
They were just walking on the beach.
The turtles' shells are crushed by the rubbish.
It is like you're destroying your own skin.
Animals are angry.
Arctic foxes are struggling with environmental pollution.
Dolphins' tails are cut by rubbish.
Birds get stuck in plastic bags.

We are killing them on the ground, in the ocean and even in the sky.
If you do this you are endangering our creatures.
Let's help animals,
This means you.

Jason Roh (10)
St Andrew's Prep, Eastbourne

Save Our Turtles

S ome day we need to make a stand
A litter picker would help us all
V ery little turtles live on this day
E veryone needs to help

O ur lives are in danger
U nbearable damage to our ocean
R ecycle plastic otherwise we'll die

T urtles are dying because of us
U nderwater swimmers need our help
R ubbish is the worst
T ell people to help, that would make a big difference
L osing turtles is heartbreaking
E ven just putting plastic in the right bin
S o help us to save the turtles.

Charlotte Millar (9)
St Andrew's Prep, Eastbourne

The Polar Bears

Ice dancers can dance no more.
Their ballroom is gone, their fun ended.
We listen to the news of the wild
But go on with no hesitation
Destroying their world.
I call to you to make a difference.
I call to you to make a stand.
Our mistakes need to be rectified, we need to save nature.
Too long have we lived in destruction and watched our planet die.
Resisting the call of the wild.
Nature needs help.
I call to you to make a difference.
I call to you to make a stand.
Save Earth. Save our planet.
One day it will be too late,
The ice dancers will dance no more.

Beatrice Porter (10)
St Andrew's Prep, Eastbourne

Climate Change

C limate change is destroying our world
L et us do something about it
I f we do not do anything
M aybe our world will be gone as we know it
A nd we would kill millions of animals
T o see our world destroyed
E nding our planet

C hange can be good but not this change
H ow is it that our planet is being destroyed?
A nd some people might not do anything about it
N ot even trying
G orillas, tigers, rhinos, anteaters, owls, fish, sharks and many more
E nd climate change now.

Teo DiPasquo (9)
St Andrew's Prep, Eastbourne

Antarctica's Ice

A ntarctica is dying
N ot cold enough to survive
T earing ice falling
A ntarctica is in danger
R ushing away to find new homes
C old weather but it is not freezing enough
T iny ice blocks on the sea
I ce is melting, not enough to live
C old weather but it is not freezing enough
A ntarctica's animals are dying
S eas are warming

I ce is not ice anymore
C old weather is moving away
E ssentially Antarctica could be gone forever.

Darcie Walton (10)
St Andrew's Prep, Eastbourne

The Big Blue Issue

From dangerous jaws to crookedly long claws.
Our planet needs help.
White rhinos, polar bears, red pandas and spider monkeys.
Our planet needs help.
Plastic bottles, napkins and tissue paper.
Our planet needs help.

I was born to a ball, it was green and blue.
Our planet needs help.
My mother and father said, "Use it wisely,
You only have one but it belongs to others too."
Our planet needs help.
You only have one life, be clever with it.
Our planet needs help.

Thomas Price (10)
St Andrew's Prep, Eastbourne

Spider Monkey

S pider monkeys are in danger
P ollinating flowers and spreading seeds is their job
I n parts of the world there are very few
D ue to destruction of their land
E ven in a forest they struggle to survive
R oles in their habitat are vital

M any hunters try to hurt the monkeys
O n trees they are not safe
N ot many can survive
K eeping these species alive is vital
E veryone needs to help
Y ou can start now!

Joe Cornford (10)
St Andrew's Prep, Eastbourne

Penguins

P ecking penguins huddling on the ice
E ndangered species
N ot enough cold water to survive
G ather more ice for the penguins
U ntil things change this is a real possibility
I ce melting in Antarctica
N ever stop trying to save them
S ave the penguins.

Charlie Walter (9)
St Andrew's Prep, Eastbourne

Gorillas

G iants of the ape world
O versized monkeys
R olling around in the forest, ripping leaves to eat
I ntelligent mammals
L olloping around
L iving in Asia
A nd endangered.

Seb Temple (10)
St Andrew's Prep, Eastbourne

Monkeys

A kennings poem

Tree swinger
Banana eater
Tail curler
Loud squealer
Tummy giggler
Rowdy climber
Messy eater
Quiet sneaker.

Saskia Elliott (9)
St Andrew's Prep, Eastbourne

Plastic In The Ocean

Animal choker
Sea destroyer
Turtles trapped
Whales dying
Rubbish throwers
Fish slicing.

Kiana Williams (10)
St Andrew's Prep, Eastbourne

The King's Coronation

Charles III is now our monarch...

C harles will be king
O ath is what he will say
R eign is what he will do
O n his head will be his crown
N ow King Charles is our king
A good representation and role model
T ill the end he will keep his promise
I n the end he will care for us
O ver the years he has waited, now his wish came true
N ow is the time to welcome our new king.

Kings are who care without hesitation
Who rule for their nation
He will be our king and start a good memory.

Sharon Osindero (9)
St Margaret's CE Primary School, Hollinwood

King Charles III's Coronation Day

K ing Charles III
I s going to be king
N ow is the time to welcome him in
G reat leader he will be

C oronation day is on the 6th May
H ard work that might be
A fter King Charles is Prince William
R ight every day
L ove is felt to be king
E lizabeth says goodbye
S ymbols of the cross.

On Saturday 6th of May
King Charles III will be crowned that day
Visitors will celebrate
So don't forget that date.

Pola Piotrowska (9)
St Margaret's CE Primary School, Hollinwood

King Charles

K ind
I nnocent
N ice
G enerous

C harming
H onest
A mazing
R adiant
L oving
E qual
S erene.

He is kind and nice
Because his mother taught him right.

He is generous and charming
Because whenever he sees homeless people
On the floor he gives them food
Because they are starving.

King Charles III is loving
Because he loves to be shaking other people's hands.

Mabel Conteh (10)
St Margaret's CE Primary School, Hollinwood

Coronation

C harles III is king on 6th May
O ath will be said by King Charles
R oyal family
O ur future king, after King Charles is Prince William
N ow is the time to welcome a new king
A mazingly, King Charles is our king
T omorrow is the coronation of King Charles
I t will be a spectacular celebration
O penness is what King Charles needs to use
N o man in the UK is greater than King Charles.

Joe Duggan (9)
St Margaret's CE Primary School, Hollinwood

Coronation Poem

C harles III's coronation
O n Saturday 6th King Charles will be crowned
R oyalty of King Charles' reign will be long
O aths for King Charles are long
N o one hates King Charles
A crown will go on King Charles' head
T o King Charles heart will be nice
I n King Charles' heart will be good
O n coronation day a lot of people come
N o one will bring hate to King Charles.

Yousaf (9)
St Margaret's CE Primary School, Hollinwood

The Coronation Poem

The Aten sun is glorious
On this most auspicious day,
The hall is decked with flowers
And banners bright like just one day.

Nobles and gentlemen from far
And near in their finery arrayed,
Representing all kingdoms
In the colours they have displayed.

In soft warm glow of candlelight,
An excited hush comes o'er the throng,
Through an arch of warrior steel
Strides the mighty crowned King Charles.

Maheen (9)
St Margaret's CE Primary School, Hollinwood

Coronation Poem

C harles III will be king
O ath is what he has to say
R espect is what he'll get
O n this day we'll celebrate
N ow people are camping near Buckingham Palace
A ll the citizens are coming
T ime to buy your flags and wave
I t's nearly time, just be patient
O ver the world we'll cheer for the new king
N ow is the day to celebrate with your friends.

Aaminah (8)
St Margaret's CE Primary School, Hollinwood

Coronation Poem

C oronation day is on the 6th of May
O ath is what he has to say
R oyalness is what he is
O n the throne he will sit
N ow is the time to welcome the new king
A mazingly King Charles III is our king
T omorrow will be the big day
I ncredibly millions of people will witness the spectacular ceremony
O peness is what he has to use
N o lies allowed.

Corey Dodman (9)
St Margaret's CE Primary School, Hollinwood

Coronation

C harles III is going to be crowned
O ath is what he has to say
R oyal he is to us
O h, incredibly London will be filled in red, white and blue
N ew monarch he is
A t Buckingham Palace he lives
T omorrow is the day
I nside Westminster Abbey it will be
O n the 6th Of May
N ow is the time to welcome a new king.

Darcy (9)
St Margaret's CE Primary School, Hollinwood

Coronation Poem

K ind person fit to be king
I nvincible individual
N ice and caring
G reat leader, wonderful king

C oronation Day on the 6th May
H is mother passed
A nd will hopefully live a long life
R oyal king
L ong live the King
E veryone will see the coronation
S top and watch the coronation.

Rayyan C Malik (9)
St Margaret's CE Primary School, Hollinwood

Coronation Poem

C oronation is on the 6th of May
O ath the King will say
R oyal colours spread around London
O h there's a new king
N ow is the time to celebrate
A nd the King will be crowned
T ea parties in the streets
I n London there were celebrations
O nly Charles can be king
N ow is the time for Charles.

Ryan (9)
St Margaret's CE Primary School, Hollinwood

Coronation Poem

C rown prince
O ne will say an oath
R oyal family
O n 6th May King Charles will become king
N ow King Charles has desserts
A new king is here
T errific fun
I n some years William will be king
O n Saturday 6th of May Charles will be king of the UK
N ow King Charles on Monday will be king.

Charlie Whalen (10)
St Margaret's CE Primary School, Hollinwood

Coronation Poem

C harles III will be crowned king
O ath is what he says
R eign is for a long time
O n the 6th of May
N ever have I seen King Charles
A lways remembered Queen Elizabeth
T he King is royalty
I sn't it amazing?
O ver the world people will be joyful
N ow King Charles will be king!

Lacey (10)
St Margaret's CE Primary School, Hollinwood

The Coronation Of The King

K ing Charles III
I s going to be king
N ot to disrespect
G oing to the throne

C oronation day is coming
H ave a crown made
A s London will have a party
R are London has fun
L ondon will want to barbecue
E lizabeth died in 2022
S ent the throne to King Charles.

Huzdifah (10)
St Margaret's CE Primary School, Hollinwood

Coronation Poem

K ind-hearted for the crown
I nspiring for children
N oble for his rule, the King
G enius to be smart

C aring for the Commonwealth
H eartfelt for people
A ngelic to the oath
R oyal family
L oyal to his people
E ager to be king
S acred coronation.

Sienna Tucker (10)
St Margaret's CE Primary School, Hollinwood

Coronation Poem: Camilla Speech I Made

As long as forever I will stay by your side.
I will be your companion,
Your friend,
Your wife.
I'll do anything for you, I'll go anywhere.
I'll bring you the sunshine, I'll comfort your fears.
As long as forever my heart will be true,
My heart will be true for as long as I live,
I'll always love you.

Joanna Osindero (9)
St Margaret's CE Primary School, Hollinwood

King Charles

K ing Charles the III
I nspiring king
N ice
G reat king

C aring for his country
H is Royal Highness
A kind king will protect his country
R eign this country
L earn from King Charles
E agerly he will become king
S tay the king.

Deen (10)
St Margaret's CE Primary School, Hollinwood

Coronation Poem

C harles III
O n 6th May it's the day
R oyal family
O n a special day he will be King of England
N ew king is now part of history
A fter 70 years
T he King is true
I ncredibly he is our king
O ath, what we have to do
N o lies anymore.

Varun (9)
St Margaret's CE Primary School, Hollinwood

Coronation Poem

C harles the III to be king
O n the 6th of May
R eign to be king
O aths are what he has to say
N ow King Charles is on the throne
A fter the Queen passed
T he King has arrived
I ntelligent king
O aths to the King
N ow welcome the King.

Antonia (10)
St Margaret's CE Primary School, Hollinwood

Coronation Day

K ind every day
I ncredibly busy
N ever mean
G ood king!

C oronation Day is on 6.5.23
H as a lot of jobs
A s good as can be
R ight every day
L oads of kindness
E veryone knows to come
S o come to Coronation Day!

Maya Pedley (9)
St Margaret's CE Primary School, Hollinwood

Coronation Poem

It's the day, the day the King will be crowned
With lots of food and fun.
Come on, come on,
Cakes and chocolate!
There is so much to be done!
There is nothing to miss.
Come on, come on!
Let's play!
Everyone is invited,
Have a crowd
And watch the King being crowned.

Lulya Tewelde (9)
St Margaret's CE Primary School, Hollinwood

Coronation Poem

Soon King Charles will become our king,
The joy, the happiness, our voices shall sing.
A golden crown shall be firmly placed on his head,
Oh yes, it's true, King Charles has been said!
The King looks so smart in red, blue and white,
Look at his outstanding robe as bright as a knight.

Divine (9)
St Margaret's CE Primary School, Hollinwood

Coronation Poem

K ing Charles will show kindness
I ncredibly in London everyone in red, white and blue
N ew king will be crowned
G reat king.

Muhammad Asfaan Rafi (8)
St Margaret's CE Primary School, Hollinwood

No Milk For Me

When I was little I wanted to be,
A person without an allergy.
It made me sad, I would cry,
But I didn't tell anyone why.
I don't know why it happened to me,
But I had to be dairy free.
I couldn't eat yoghurt or ice cream,
To eat chocolate was my big dream.
There were lots of foods I could now find
And all my friends were really kind.
Lucky for me when I grew,
I could have milk by Year 2.
Some kids don't grow out of allergies, they never get a rest,
I hope they are okay because they are the best.
When I am big,
I want to be a person who cures allergies!

Matilda Davey (8)
St Martin's Preparatory School, Grimsby

Song Of The Waves

A young boy gazed out of his window
Eating a hot flaky chicken pie out of the oven.
Bedtime called, but he wasn't sleepy,
Instead he watched the ocean tell its story.
Crash, went the waves on the lighthouse which shone
Like a dazzling torch out to the dark night.
He tiptoed as quiet as a mouse out of the shiny,
Golden door into another dimension.
One hundred old crooked barrels lay like dead fish
In the sizzling sand beneath his feet.
The boy's dream about smugglers hadn't been a dream at all.

Otto Gabriel Johnson (7)
St Martin's Preparatory School, Grimsby

Today I Get To Relax

Today is the 5th of May!
Now I get to play if I have a say.
There is still a lot of rain
Which is a big pain.
I hope it will be sunny
So then I will hop with my pet bunny.
My dog called Gini,
I hope she hasn't seen me.
My cat is called Lilly.
My best friend is called Billy.
Myself,
I have an elf
But I knocked it off the shelf.
My dad,
I hope he won't be mad.
At least my mum is the opposite of sad.
I went to sleep
And wished I had a pet sheep.

Reeva Raghwani (8)
St Martin's Preparatory School, Grimsby

Maisie And Me

My dog Maisie is furry and small.
She loves to go out and play with her ball.
Maisie likes to have fun in the sun,
She is so fast when we go on a run.
I love Maisie because she is crazy
But when she's in bed she is very lazy.
Sometimes Maisie is very sweet,
When she is good she gets a treat.
In the night when it is dark
Maisie will let out a mighty bark.
Mum will say, "What was that?"
Dad will say, "Probably a cat."

Mollie Simmons (8)
St Martin's Preparatory School, Grimsby

Beach Emotions

The seaweed washes,
I feel weird,
The boats are fast,
I feel peaceful.

The fish are yummy,
I feel hungry,
The sun is hot,
I feel sweaty.

The sea crashes,
I feel satisfied,
The sand is soft,
I feel calm.

The trees are wavy,
I feel dizzy,
The grass is tickly,
I feel giggly.

The treasure is big,
I feel excited,
The shells are pearly,
I feel ecstatic.

I am on the beach,
I feel happy.

Spencer Stead (8)
St Martin's Preparatory School, Grimsby

My Dad

Dad looked cool
Sitting by the pool
Eating pickles
And getting the tickles

And got salt and pepper
Then got busy writing a letter
And then put on his top
To go to the shop

And got some soap
Then got in a mope
He got sick
Then got hit by a brick.

Aaria Bhullar (7)
St Martin's Preparatory School, Grimsby

Winter Emotions

The reindeer run,
I feel relaxed,
The mountains are snowy,
I feel calm,
The trees creak,
I feel annoyed,
The wind whooshes through the trees,
I feel disturbed,
The huskies howl,
I feel scared,
The sleigh has presents in it,
I feel joyful.

Emilie-Grace Roe (8)
St Martin's Preparatory School, Grimsby

My Football Poem

Football makes me happy.
If only I had legs as fast as Mbappé,
The skills of Ronaldo are like nothing I've seen
Haaland's goals are super clean.
I have mastered the Maradona turn in training
Even when it's raining!

Noah Kolomashin (8)
St Martin's Preparatory School, Grimsby

Pollution

Pollution! Pollution! Pollution!
We must all try to find the solution!
Grown-ups and children,
We need to think what to do about it every day!
To save our beautiful world,
We all have an important part to play.
Remember!

Nikolaos Oplopoiadis (8)
St Martin's Preparatory School, Grimsby

My Guitar

I play the Les Paul electric guitar,
I am a super famous rockstar!

I have a top hat that I wear,
I have big black curly hair!

My guitar skills on November Rain,
Are well and truly insane!

Who am I?

Elliott Wright (8)
St Martin's Preparatory School, Grimsby

Emotions

The trees rustle
I feel scared
The sky is bright
I feel light
The stars are beautiful
I feel calm
The birds are sly
I feel happy
Ghosts are close
I feel jittery
The branches slide
I feel sad.

Rosie Blake (8)
St Martin's Preparatory School, Grimsby

I'm A Little Doggy

I'm a little doggy,
Small and black,
I have small white spots
And a fluffy tail.
When I get excited
I will bark.
Grab the ball
And let's go to the park.

Marley Dunham (8)
St Martin's Preparatory School, Grimsby

A Portal To A Strange Land

Hidden in the alley of Blueberry Lane,
Is a portal waiting to be used,
It's rainbow and glittery with smoke all around.
Who knew? No one in the town.
On the other side of this marvellous thing,
The very strange people like to sing.
They are all very short with purple skin like little plums,
They walk around in dungarees with butterfly patches on their knees.
All the cities are very fun like the sweet one,
Cotton candy clouds, a chocolate river,
Gingerbread houses and candy cane fences.
Yes, there is a paper city with paper everywhere,
There are paper houses, towers, trees, even wildlife is paper.
There's one very dangerous indeed
With witches lurking in the trees.
Other than that it's very fun.

Isabella Welfare (10)
St Mary's Catholic Primary School, Salterbeck

Nature Blooms

Flowers blooming from the glistening emerald-green grass as huge trees sprout.
Meanwhile, mushrooms leap from the ground!
One squirrel and another running about among weeds
and flowers as rivers and lakes dance along.
Birds sang while the grass went with the flow of the wind,
as bees flew past the grumpy clouds.
Diamond-blue water trickled down the waterfall,
past the sprouting trees, strangling the land.
The flowers skipped around ignoring the clouds' complaints as they rather would shout or mumble.
Dandelions skipped as roses tickled the ground,
Lotus flowers lying while daisies
and buttercups sat on their roots.
All of them consider themselves beautiful as parts of our nature.

Mila Taylor-Kennedy (10)
St Mary's Catholic Primary School, Salterbeck

Wonderful Nature

The trees stood as tall as a skyscraper.
The trees strangled the air.
The huge tree was like a wiggly worm.

Birds flew in the bright sky.
They sang and sang all day long.
They danced in the sky and flapped their beautiful wings.

The pretty, colourful flowers swayed left and right in the wind.
They danced like little people.
They danced all day long.

The bright yellow sun shone down at the water.
It was shining down all day long.

The beautiful water rowed down the waterfall gently.
Fish and ducks swam all day long.

Amelia Briley (9)
St Mary's Catholic Primary School, Salterbeck

Funny Riddles

What is green,
Points up the sky
And is almost everywhere in the world?
Grass.

What is dark,
A tiny space
And underground?
A coffin.

I have no arms,
But I have legs
And long ears.
What am I?
An elephant.

it is huge and caring
And helps you every day,
It's giant and red.
What is it?
A heart.

What do you call someone that's got no nose
And no body?
Nobody knows!

What do you call
Something that's black, white and red?
A blushing penguin rolling down a hill.

Danny Hilferty (10)
St Mary's Catholic Primary School, Salterbeck

Veruca Salt

Spending money very fast,
Running around like a little brat.
"I need another holiday abroad!"
"Okay Veruca, my darling."
All the money in the world
Just to be a spoilt girl!
"I want a golden ticket."
"Here you go you little brat,
Someone needs to teach you how to act!"
When Veruca says buy,
It's like a battle cry.
Using money to wipe her tears,
Wiping the sweat from her ears.
Down the rubbish chute, she goes,
When she is back she is covered in...
"Ew! Gross!"

Mylee Weston (10)
St Mary's Catholic Primary School, Salterbeck

Dreams

In some people's dreams, they never give up!
Always try your best!
In some people's dreams,
They dream about being a dancer
And finally finding an answer.
In some people's dreams, they are doing maths in their baths!
In some people's dreams, they are speeding so fast in a Ferrari
Like children on a wild safari.
Dream, dream, dream just keep on dreaming.
In some people's dreams, they don't give up!
Try your best, never give up!
Dream, dream, dream, just keep on dreaming!
Finally, wake up.

Amira-Lily Plater (10)
St Mary's Catholic Primary School, Salterbeck

The Falling Dream

One day I started drawing
But everyone started falling.
I said, "Was it magic?"
But suddenly it was very tragic.
When I was playing rugby everyone did the same thing,
I then saw God and he gave me a wink,
He said, "Go hide, go run,"
And I said, "Actually this is fun."
Then I woke up on a beam
And I said, "Oh, it was all a dream."

Sonny Adams (10)
St Mary's Catholic Primary School, Salterbeck

Funny Football

F ootball is fun and sunny and it gives you loads of exercise
O verpower a piece of sun and helps you run a lot
O n the other hand, people think that it is like you're on the moon
T asks and telling people what to do
B all, bouncy and very funny
A sking and asking for the ball
L aughter and loads of fun
L oud all day long.

Kye Metherell (10)
St Mary's Catholic Primary School, Salterbeck

Bag-Astrophy

You can carry me when I am light,
Other times, I'm as heavy as three footballs,
I am openable unless I have been packed a little overflowing!
I can contain many items such as water bottles and more.
I am used to carry shopping, a piece of paper or even a jacket.
I am used at school to carry water bottles, books and homework.
I am taken on trips.
What am I?

Oliver Carruthers (10)
St Mary's Catholic Primary School, Salterbeck

Drama

D o not get on the wrong side of me
R umours, rumours, girl, you're enough!
A rgh, she has got knickers on her head
M ore and more I heard, "She's a spoilt brat!" How is this fear?
A lmost happy but they can't get envious. Can we all just be happy for one moment?

Gracie Nugent (10)
St Mary's Catholic Primary School, Salterbeck

My House

My giant jiggly house,
Like the jelly in my belly,
That I ate on a plate with a silver spoon.

In the house,
My brother slurped and burped a Pot Noodle,
While I had fun eating a bun.

My mum is always sleeping,
While dreaming about how life would be nice
If we didn't have mice.

Layla Agnew (10)
St Mary's Catholic Primary School, Salterbeck

Friends

F riends are there for you when you need them. They make you feel better
R eturn of your friend after everything
I like to play football with my friends
E verywhere I go I am joyful and happy
N eeds for the people who are ill
D ogs are my favourite animal in the world.

Amelia Dunleavy (10)
St Mary's Catholic Primary School, Salterbeck

Football

Football, football in the air.
Football, football in my hair.
Football, football on my head.
Football, football on my shoe.
Football, football goes to shoot.
Football, football scored for you.
One on zero, now we've won.
One on zero, now we're one.

Kenzie Sibbald (10)
St Mary's Catholic Primary School, Salterbeck

Swimming

I am splashing,
Everybody is laughing,
I don't know why but it's kind of annoying.
I am drifting,
Everybody is lifting...
I swam across the crystal-clear pool.
Everybody watched me,
It was terrific
Or even tragic.

Courtney Hefford (10)
St Mary's Catholic Primary School, Salterbeck

Dog Art

This little doggy
With a little body,
Jumped on the couch,
Sneezed once or twice,
The humans said, "No!"
He hopped on the window,
Pressed his wet nose on it
And drew proudly until, "No!"

Tilly Scott (10)
St Mary's Catholic Primary School, Salterbeck

The Lonely House

My house is made of beautiful candyfloss.
My house is as green as a mountain
Of glistening, lovely trees singing.
My house is as tall as a herd of cows.
My house is as lovely as an animal zoo.
My house is the best.

Summer Dummigan (9)
St Mary's Catholic Primary School, Salterbeck

Animal Castle

C at on top with human
A flamingo for a statue
S pider for a trap
T all monkey for a guard
L eopard for a painting
E lephant for walls.

Luke McAllister (10)
St Mary's Catholic Primary School, Salterbeck

Why Is It So Hard?

I'm hard,
I hurt you when you step on me.
You can build with me.
I don't have legs or arms.
I'm not alive.
What am I?

Answer: Lego.

Raine Sharpe (10)
St Mary's Catholic Primary School, Salterbeck

What Am I?

I am in your house.
I travel with you everywhere.
You need me to go out
And stay in.
What am I?

Answer: Underwear.

Liam Dryden (10)
St Mary's Catholic Primary School, Salterbeck

The Coronation

On the 6th May,
Is a cheerful coronation day.
London is alive with colours red, white and blue,
Commonwealth flags and bunting too.
All generations are gathered together,
The rain pours down - it's soggy wet weather.
Standing so long to catch a glimpse of the King,
The crowds unite with each other and begin to sing.
British and Commonwealth soldiers march proud,
Trumpets blowing and drums banging loud.
As the golden carriage strolls along,
The elegant horses pull slow and strong.
King Charles walks gracefully into the Abbey with his long red robe,
People are watching all around the globe.
He receives his two sceptres, orb and sword,
The holy oil is carefully poured.
The crown is placed upon his head with shimmering gems and jewels,
Three cheers for Charles, a new king rules.

Brendan Brown (10)
St Wilfrid's Catholic Primary School, Hartford

All About Marcus Rashford

R ashford is a great footballer and an inspiration to others, he has been awarded an MBE by the Queen.

A mazing footballer! With Manchester United Marcus has numerous awards and trophies.

S aving lives. As well as being an inspiration on the pitch, Rashford has told the government to give free meals.

H ungry people. Marcus wrote to the government to give free school meals to people who can't afford it.

F acing the Queen, Rashford was awarded an MBE for his charity work in 2021.

O ctober 31st 1997, Rashford was born making him only 24 when he was awarded his MBE.

R eaching for justice. During Covid there were no free school meals but Rashford jumped in and changed everything.

D ifficult early life. When he was younger his mum worked several jobs so she could feed the family.

Mark Thompson (9)
St Wilfrid's Catholic Primary School, Hartford

The Environment

Our oceans are filling with plastic and waste,
To save our seas we must make haste.
Our sealife is choking, there's no time to wait.
They must not be left in the hands of fate.

Fires are roaring through the Amazon rainforest.
The Earth is warming, this year is the hottest.
Villages and homes are being cleared and burned,
These lessons now need to be learned.

Pollution fills the air,
This is just not fair.
The future generation is in our hands,
We should start making new green plans.

But the world still has hope to stop pollution,
Repair the damage with my solution.
Solar power, wind power, thermal heat from the ground,
Alternatives to fossil fuels are all around.

Let's get together, make a change today -
This surely can be the only way!

Sarah Baylis (10)
St Wilfrid's Catholic Primary School, Hartford

Could England Do It?

Tension was rising,
I felt nervous,
The day came when England had to play France.
It was the quarter-finals of the World Cup,
Just seventeen minutes in France had made it 1-0,
I was devastated,
Then there was hope,
All Harry Kane needed was a penalty,
So he didn't let his country down.
1-1, we still had a chance,
78 minutes passed, we all thought it was going to penalties,
But France struck again.
2-1, the whole country thought the dream was over,
Then Harry Kane had one last chance to be a hero, we got a pen,
All the pressure was on him,

Running up to the ball, hit it, but it was just over the bar.
The whole country sat there disappointed.
England went home.

Oscar Rowling (10)
St Wilfrid's Catholic Primary School, Hartford

The Friends Acrostic Poem

F or real friends make you laugh and help you in sticky situations and you can tell anything to them and they keep it secret

R ing your friends if you can and if you're down they will cheer you up

I think my friends are perfect with the friendship rules and follow it well

E verlasting friendship to last all the days of your life

N o friendships should be short or should have a lot and I mean a lot of arguing in it or it's a fake friend

D ifferent friends come from different backgrounds but any person from any background that wants to be your friend, at least try and become his/her friend

S pecial friends are always there for you and have your back in any situation.

Taylor Hughes (10)
St Wilfrid's Catholic Primary School, Hartford

A Friend...

A friend is like a shining star that twinkles and glows
Or maybe like a crystal-cold ocean that gently flows.
A friend is like shining gold that you should keep in your heart and treasure
And take care forever and ever.
A friend is like a guardian angel that is there to guide you.
A friend is someone I can trust out of a few.
A friend is more than a million,
They are one of a special kind.
They give you all you need (smile).
They will be by your side every minute of every hour of the day.
Friendship...
Friendship is everything,
It's all you need.

Kornelia Ciborowski (10)
St Wilfrid's Catholic Primary School, Hartford

I Love School

I love school, it's really cool,
It is really amazing when they have a pool.
I love my teacher Mrs Hughes,
She makes me laugh when I look confused.
I love my school friends, we all play together,
We never leave anyone out 'cause we're best friends forever!
I love to work and learn new skills,
So when I get older I can pay my bills.
I love being a part of St Wilfrid's School,
My journey isn't over yet but that's still cool.
I'll be in Year 6 soon, which will be like heaven
But before you know it I'll be in Year 7.

Tiarna Murphy (10)
St Wilfrid's Catholic Primary School, Hartford

A Dragon Who Wanted To Rule The World

A dragon who wanted to rule the world
Would be fierce and strong
And do no wrong.
Puffed out chest, flared nostrils
And a glint in his eye,
No one will cross him or they will die.
Mighty powers come from him,
And he will rule the world with everyone in.
A knight called Jack, with a shield on his back,
With courage and might he swore he would fight,
the fire-breathing dragon.
They soon realised, that being friends was much better,
And made a promise to find a way, to all live happily together.

Aidan Broady (10)
St Wilfrid's Catholic Primary School, Hartford

Strawberry

From a bush growing flowers,
Blossoming towers and towers.

Being a flower was new,
But there will be something to do.

Folding and squishing petals go,
After a month a fruit will grow.

Green and small not to eat,
But the time needs to repeat.

Months will go as the berries grow,
It will be good to eat, the farmer will know.

Red and fresh hanging off the bush
And in the end, it disappears with a whoosh!

Krzysztof Nathan Kamranczyk (9)
St Wilfrid's Catholic Primary School, Hartford

The Coronation

C rowned, he was made king
O ur king
R uns our country
O ur country shouldn't hate him
N obody should hurt his feelings
A person that should be shown respect (he shall not be hated)
T he loved king
I s the son of the Queen
O ther people from different countries come to watch this fantastic moment
N obody thought that this would happen until it came to this day.

Jacob Appleton (10)
St Wilfrid's Catholic Primary School, Hartford

When I Write...

When I write a story...
My imagination swirls,
Like a dancing ballerina,
Swirling and twirling,
Until I find the plot.
When I write a poem,
I think extra deep,
As deep as a bottomless pit.
Deeper, deeper,
It's almost never-ending.
When I write anything,
I put my mind to it,
Make my handwriting all fancy,
Think of what I've written,
Laugh and smile,
What a happy ending...

Lilly Whiston (10)
St Wilfrid's Catholic Primary School, Hartford

Our World

If the sun stops shining
The trees will start to sway
And the birds will start dining
Before tucking snuggly away.

The owls and foxes come to play
Under the carpet of twinkling stars
They have slept comfortably all day
In the forest behind the monkey bars.

Now the moon comes out eagerly
Shining like a precious pearl
Bunnies are hopping speedily
As they practise their favourite twirls.

Anna Leavy (10)
St Wilfrid's Catholic Primary School, Hartford

You Don't Have To Be Perfect

There is no such thing as perfect.
The perfect family, the perfect job, the perfect house, the perfect life.
Not a single person is perfect.
We all did wrong things and we learned from them.
We have a choice to make happiness spread all over the beautiful world.
But being perfect might cause unhappiness.
Just be yourself, don't let anyone stop you.
Be happy, not perfect.

Sophia Zeta (10)
St Wilfrid's Catholic Primary School, Hartford

Horse Riding

Beautiful and majestic, naughty and nice.
Horses rattle your mind from left and right.
They walk or trot whether you like it or not,
Hold on tight or they'll give you a fright.
They like to eat hay
Before they go out and play.
They run with their friends
And kick their back ends.

I love horses because they are great
And I want one as my best mate.

Tess Lucas (10)
St Wilfrid's Catholic Primary School, Hartford

Our King

King Charles our nature-loving king born in 1949,
Reign over us every day until the next king rules over the land.

King Charles our kind soul sits on his throne and watches over us
From his palace as he signs papers and pictures.

King Charles our king, our one and only king,
He looks after us like we are his children
As we say, "God save the King!"

Mason-Adam Brown (10)
St Wilfrid's Catholic Primary School, Hartford

People Who Are Special To Me

A recipe about my mum,
Full of love and kisses,
Enough kindness and support
To fill a million dishes.

Preheat the oven with love,
Make the batter that's made from:
A stick of support
A sprinkle of kindness
A tbsp of love
Then add condensed fun
Bake in the oven for 20 minutes
And *bam*, you have the best mum.

Gabriella Proctor (10)
St Wilfrid's Catholic Primary School, Hartford

Coronation

C rowning a new king
O ur voice for the nation
R eigning over the UK
O ur King, Charles III
N ature lover, looking after our planet
A follower of God
T imes will change
I believe he'll be good
O n his throne he will rule
N ow until it's time to pass his crown.

Ben Watts (10)
St Wilfrid's Catholic Primary School, Hartford

When I Grow Up

When I grow up
I won't hide behind boulders
Like worried soldiers.

When I grow up
I won't try to look finer
Like gold miners.

When I grow up
Maybe I'll be like superstars
Buying fancy fast cars.

When I grow up
I will be like engineers
Always fixing gears!

Alisha Tomlinson (10)
St Wilfrid's Catholic Primary School, Hartford

Fangirl

I know that I will never meet you.
To you, I'm just another fan,
But to me...
You're my inspiration,
You're my idol,
You're my world.
I know that I will never meet you...
But I will support you
As you're half spirit.
You... through thick and thin.

I love you...

Sayanthana S (10)
St Wilfrid's Catholic Primary School, Hartford

The Love Poem

Roses are red
Violets are blue
I don't love you or maybe I do.

My love for you is too strong
But you just count it as a bond
How did it come to this?

I wish for our love to be strong
It's sad we don't get along
'Cause I thought we had a bond.

I love you!

Bradley Tomlinson (10)
St Wilfrid's Catholic Primary School, Hartford

The King's Coronation

To the King on his special day,
I wish him good luck
And hope he doesn't feel any dismay.
I'm sure all he can think about is the crown being put on his head
Or maybe even getting into bed.
All in all Charles,
I wish you the best
And can't wait for Prince Louis to make a big mess.

Jessica Leigh (9)
St Wilfrid's Catholic Primary School, Hartford

School Is Not So Cool

School, school, school,
A school is not so cool.
We're here for five days a week,
Six hours a day.

School, school, school,
A school is not so cool.
People laugh when we fall,
We must have to make a call.

School, school, school,
A school is not so cool.

Ava Child (10)
St Wilfrid's Catholic Primary School, Hartford

My BFF

F orever you will look out for me
R eally listens when I have a problem
I can talk to her when she is feeling sad
E ats her dinner with me all the time to keep each other company
N ever fall out with each other
D efinitely, always best friends together.

Esme Strong (10)
St Wilfrid's Catholic Primary School, Hartford

Nature

Everything is nature,
God has given us a feature.
Nature isn't a toy,
It is joy.
The sun is shining,
The sky is blue.
The birds are flying,
High up in the valleys.
With green trees and buzzing bees,
The grass is so green and everything is so clean.

Aimey Kiran (10)
St Wilfrid's Catholic Primary School, Hartford

Doctor Who (TARDIS)

T ime is all The Doctor has in his big blue box
A nd with his companions to help
R elative to the time or planet The Doctor arrives at
D imension, Rose gets trapped in a parallel one
I n a moment, run!
S pace, the infinite universe.

Thomas Burston (10)
St Wilfrid's Catholic Primary School, Hartford

How To Make A True Friend

Preheat the oven with warm hugs
And sprinkles of friendship,
Served with plenty of happiness.
Bake with tender love and care
And all the things you share,
This is a must.
Enjoy the cake but don't eat it fast
So it'll last just like friendship.

Ethan Coot (10)
St Wilfrid's Catholic Primary School, Hartford

Friends

F orever until the end
R eal as real can be
I ncredible times together
E verlasting memories
N one judging but smiling friends
D azzling everywhere they go
S unshine because you are the light I need.

Layla Barlow (10)
St Wilfrid's Catholic Primary School, Hartford

Monkey In The Forest

Monkeys swinging between the vines,
Herds of elephants passing by,
Stomping as loud as a mammoth's step,
Birds are frightened and flee their nests,
Crocodiles in the river stretch up to peep,
Careless monkeys jump and leap.

Oliver Ho (10)
St Wilfrid's Catholic Primary School, Hartford

A Riddle

I am a light source
And require no batteries.
I need to be shaken to be changed.
What am I?

Answer: A Shake Light flashlight.

Marshall Meenan (10)
St Wilfrid's Catholic Primary School, Hartford

The Tower Of Goldsacks

In the forest far away
Lived a family called the Goldsacks.
They lived in a tower with a giant flower,
A very strong power was outside the tower.
They loved that flower so much
And one of them had a power just like the flower.
The person who had the power like the flower was Maur.
She loved her power, it was telekinesis,
But not any kind of telekinesis,
It could light up the flower outside the tower
And that flower is really hard to light.
She can only use her fist or wrist.
"Hey you, I live in a tower and I have a power," said Maur.
"Yeah I know Maur, you have a power and live in a tower," said Briar, Maur's friend.

Sienna Goldsack (8)
Townhill Junior School, Townhill Park

Just Me!

So much laughter,
With my friends.
These are bonds
Which never end.

I have a fab dad
And an amazing mum too.
And two little sisters,
Such a nasty crew.

My idol is
Roald Dahl
As I want to be a writer
And make sure my books aren't dull.

My favourite treat
Is vanilla cake
And for a drink,
A vanilla milkshake.

I'm good at English,
I'm good at art.
I love equations
On a maths chart.

Ivy Salmon (10)
Townhill Junior School, Townhill Park

Team Of Friends

I have a crew of friends from a list top to bottom,
So many friends will never be forgotten.
We have picnics in the park
And like to play until dark.
We eat snacks every day
Together after we play.
We cheer for others,
Including our sisters and brothers.
We stay together,
Best friends forever and ever.

Jasmine Allen (9)
Townhill Junior School, Townhill Park

Our Tower

In this high tower
No one's ever seen
The tower's powers
Are beyond the sea,
Beware of the magic
You will see in the Atlantic sea!
There are three haunted people that roam,
The haunted creatures,
They will feed day by day
Until the day has come!
The tower!

Jessica Howard (9) & Sofia
Townhill Junior School, Townhill Park

Magical Land

M agic everywhere
A dventure eyes
G row here
I dols over there
C ool people
A ll around
L ong lives

L and here and there
A fun day
N o sleep
D o not leave.

Orla Salmon (9)
Townhill Junior School, Townhill Park

One Day

One day I hope these things could come true,
Let me list them out to you.
One day I hope everyone will stop hunting,
And I'll decorate with pretty bunting.
One day I hope everyone will stop polluting,
Hopefully, I'll be able to protest solitary.
One day let's save the orcas,
I'll raise money by becoming one of the workers.
One day I hope to stop segregation
So that everyone can be one united nation.
One day I hope to stop climate change,
So animals can stay safe in the Arctic range.
One day I hope that people will stop cutting down trees,
So that we can have lovely picnics under their shady leaves.
One day I hope all of my dreams will come true,
If you put your mind to it,
You *can* make it happen for you.

Elan Evans (9)
Ysgol Gymraeg Y Fenni, Abergavenny

Adulthood

When I grow up I want to be an author and a poem writer.
I'm so excited to be an adult but my mum says otherwise.
I don't know why she says that it's hard to be an adult,
I could watch the sunrise every morning.
I would make bedtime stories for children which would be impossible for some to find boring!
I could play with my children all day long and of course, starting at the crack of dawn!

I could make breakfast in the morning, then my children could do some drawing.
I could make cookies all day while my children go out to play.
I could meet my one true love while sitting on Cloud Nine, way up above.
I could find new recipes and make precious memories.

Sigh...
When I grow up...

Noni Pook (10)
Ysgol Gymraeg Y Fenni, Abergavenny

Red Dragon Rules

This is Wales, our beautiful home!
We'll give you a tour and then you can explore!
Like Liverpool said 'You'll never walk alone'.

First of all at Ysgol Gymraeg Y Fenni,
In the spotlight you'll find great friends
And teachers with a smile that's bright.

I play football and I love Man United
And that's my opinion,
There are other teams you may support
That are supported by millions!

We think positively, we support and welcome you
And we'll make sure, you have a great time too!
If anything happens we'll make sure you're fine
Just remember, the red dragon rules!

Maddison Edwards (10)
Ysgol Gymraeg Y Fenni, Abergavenny

How I Feel Now...

Sometimes I feel like I want to quit but I try not to.
Sometimes I feel like everyone hates me but then I don't think they do.

Sometimes I feel like there's no point in doing this or doing that.
Sometimes I feel that when I say 'no' I'm mean and I feel sorry but unseen.

Sometimes I feel like everyone is perfect and I'm not,
But then I say to myself, "Everyone is perfect in their own way!"

Sometimes I feel like I'm the odd one out
And I say, "But everyone's unique, without a doubt!"

Marisa Santiago (11)
Ysgol Gymraeg Y Fenni, Abergavenny

Happy Light Poem

Love is the light that guides you through the night,
Shining so bright, it wraps around you so tight.
Family are always there, even if they're not.
Do you know how?
Well, here's how.
I know they're in your heart,
All animals know this when they lose their young,
Or when a little cub loses its mum.
All friends know this when they move school,
So when it happens they always keep their cool.
So remember this simple rule, to help you keep your cool,
I know you'll remember this,
Soon now your life is simply bliss.

Rhonwen Croft (9)
Ysgol Gymraeg Y Fenni, Abergavenny

Nature's Sky

I picture fresh green trees
And no rubbish in the seas.
The beauty of the flower's bloom,
No leaf is in doom,
Too bad nature's sky is in a disease!

The whole world is in trouble,
Now with pollution, it costs double!
We should help since we are so smart,
Everyone should take part,
Help nature's sky or we will crumble!

We should at least try,
Make trees so birds can forever fly.
We will make the world better,
If we take care of nature together.
Thank you for helping nature's sky!

Izzy Williams (11)
Ysgol Gymraeg Y Fenni, Abergavenny

Travelling The World In A Significant Way

Day one was beautiful
Travelling through the world
Finding a dragon
To fly up and up!

Asking myself the same question,
Is this the beginning or is this devastation?
Soaring through the skies in an elegant way,
It's turned dark, day two is on its way!

Flying on my dragon's back,
Feeling the wind on my skin,
I felt something hit me hard,
Right on my shin.

Remembered when I was a child,
I wanted to see the world,
But I fell off my dragon,
Not succeeding, just burned!

Elis Dickenson (10)
Ysgol Gymraeg Y Fenni, Abergavenny

We Are Not Alone

Off on a journey to an endless realm,
Such a land to explore,
I feel so overwhelmed,
But I want to see more...

Shooting through the sky,
In a rocket way up high.
The stars shine bright,
In the deep night.

Floating under the endless sky,
I feel light as a feather.
I'm going to fly,
I feel so much better!

After years of research, we finally got it right,
This is such a flight,
But there's a hole staring at me,
Now everything is gone, goodnight.

Maisie Strong (10)
Ysgol Gymraeg Y Fenni, Abergavenny

Cheslin Kolbe

Cheslin Kolbe is my favourite rugby player,
I respect him so very much,
I love to watch his talent and skills,
He scores great tries with every touch.

Cheslin Kolbe is known for his sidestep
And his strength, speed and skill.
He scored a try in the World Cup final,
I cheered and thought, *you are so brill!*

Cheslin Kolbe plays for South Africa,
Number 14 and on the wing for Toulon,
He is quite small for a rugby player
But determination and talent have made him strong.

Celt Thomas (9)
Ysgol Gymraeg Y Fenni, Abergavenny

Mystery Murders

Jake was in the garden asleep,
While someone was having a creep.
Then minutes later,
He was killed by a traitor.

He was not found until hours after,
People think it was the enchanter.
Police started an investigation,
But they didn't find any information.

They never found out who it is,
It was like a quiz!
They found many rings,
It's not over until someone sings.

It is still a mystery to this day,
In the garden he lay.

Evie Hollister (10)
Ysgol Gymraeg Y Fenni, Abergavenny

When I Grow Up!

When I grow up I want to be beautiful,
When I grow up I want to be stronger,
When I grow up I want to be braver,
When I grow up I want to be better,
When I grow up I want to be lovelier,
When I grow up I want to be kinder,
That's what I want to be.

When I grow up I want to have a house full of animals,
And a family full of love.
When I grow up I want to have love for myself,
That's all I want to be,
When I grow up I want to be me.

Eira Lewis (10)
Ysgol Gymraeg Y Fenni, Abergavenny

The Mystical Mummies

Feast your eyes upon the pharaoh,
See if you can hear his echo,
The worshipped rich king,
Who knows how he was feeling?

The poor young Tutankhamun,
Clearly wasn't very immune,
The poor young king who is now a mummy,
His life was clearly quite bumpy.

The explorers enter the tomb,
Vulnerable to the doom,
But then with his last breath,
"Goodbye," Tutankhamun said, "this is my death."

Phoebe Evans (9)
Ysgol Gymraeg Y Fenni, Abergavenny

How I Found A Friend

It's my first day of school,
I'm a bit lonely,
I'm not very cool,
Or popular - I need a friend!

"Hello!" a shy voice cries,
Through the day, to the end.
Suddenly, I look through her eyes,
Her name, it comes to me!

I now go home, very happy,
I'm glad I found a friend,
Her name is Elepea,
We are the best friends ever!

Lucy Charrington (10)
Ysgol Gymraeg Y Fenni, Abergavenny

The Blorenge Oak

I am the oak
Watching over the world,
Standing strong and tall,
Letting no one over my turf,
I am the oak,
I look over the land,
Watching over them all,
I am the oak,
I am very old but strong,
Standing for so long,
I am the oak,
I have history and stories,
Character and personality,
I am the oak.

Flo Park (11)
Ysgol Gymraeg Y Fenni, Abergavenny

The Fairy Forest And The Dragon

In a fairy village bright,
Lived creatures small, with wings so light.
A dragon came and caused such fear,
But a brave fairy showed kindness dear.

The dragon promised to protect
And peace and joy were what they had in check.
Forever the scariest of beasts,
Can have a heart that beats and beats.

Rhoswen Jones (9)
Ysgol Gymraeg Y Fenni, Abergavenny

Flowers

Flowers, flowers everywhere,
In the garden, in my hair.
Bright and pretty all the year,
Bringing a lot of love and cheer.
Special flowers, how I like them,
They are such a cheerful sight to see all day.
All the colours, the flowers you can see,
Make me happy as can be.

Kayla Gerhardt (9)
Ysgol Gymraeg Y Fenni, Abergavenny